Belongs To:
Princess

Made in the USA
Monee, IL
02 May 2022

95787278R00068